THE SUPER SCIENCE BOOK OF WEATHER

Kay Davies and Wendy Oldfield

Weather Knows What Next

Weather comes and weather goes
With freezing fingers or red hot toes,
You think you know what to expect
But you never know what's coming next.

Illustrations by Frances Lloyd

Thomson Learning
New York

Titles in the Super Science series

Light
Our Bodies
Time
Weather

First published in the
United States in 1993 by
Thomson Learning
115 Fifth Avenue
New York, NY 10003

First published in 1992 by
Wayland (Publishers) Ltd

Library of Congress Cataloging-in-Publication Data applied for

ISBN: 1-56847-021-5
Printed in Italy

Series Editor: Cally Chambers
Designer: Loraine Hayes Design

Picture acknowledgments:

Illustrations by Frances Lloyd.
Cover illustration by Martin Gordon.

Photographs by permission of: J. Allan Cash 5, 11;
Cephas 24; Bruce Coleman Ltd. 13 Bottom (Taylor),
17 bottom, 21 (Meyers), 22 bottom (Lankinen); Ecoscene 23,
26; Environmental Picture Library 29 (Holmes); Eye
Ubiquitous 8; PHOTRI 22; top, 27 bottom, Science Photo
Library 19, 27 top; Tony Stone Worldwide 4, 13 top, 16, 17
top, 18, 25; Werner Forman Archive 28.

CONTENTS

Weather 4
Atmosphere 5
Sun Rays 6
Climate 7
Moving Air 8
Pressure Changes 9
Windy Weather 10
The Water Cycle 12
Dew Point 13
Damp Air 14
Cloud Cover 15
Thunder and Lightning 16
Violent Storms 17
Ice Cold 18
Changing Seasons 20
Migration 21
Time and Change 22
People and Weather 24
Weathering 25
Predicting the Weather 26
Weather Technology 27
Changing the Weather 28

Glossary 30
Books to Read 31
Index 32

WEATHER

People always want to know what the weather will be like. They may be planning a picnic or barbecue, or deciding how to travel to work and whether to carry an umbrella. They can listen to weather forecasts on the TV and radio. The forecasts are updated all the time, just as weather conditions are always changing and developing.

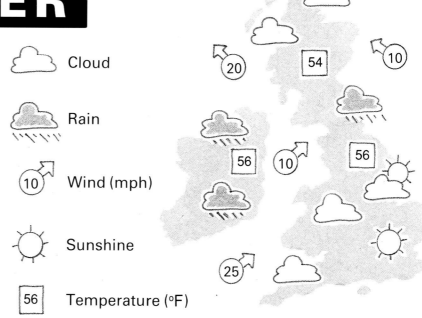

Cloud

Rain

Wind (mph)

Sunshine

56 Temperature (°F)

▲ A weather map in a newspaper can tell people what kind of weather to expect. A few simple symbols make it easy to understand.

Weather is the condition of the atmosphere around us. We see and feel the weather in the wind, rain, sunshine, frost, or fog.

◄ The weather can change quickly – a bright, sunny day can suddenly be clouded over by a dark thunderstorm. Sometimes people who are in sunny weather can see a heavy rain shower on its way.

ATMOSPHERE

The earth is surrounded by air, which is a mixture of gases that makes up the atmosphere. This mixture is mainly nitrogen and oxygen, with a small amount of carbon dioxide, a few other gases, and water vapor. Small amounts of dust and dirt are also in the air.

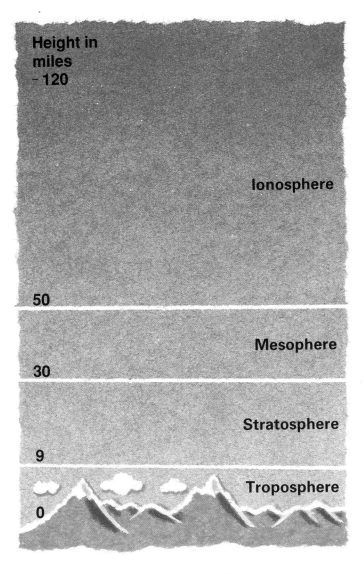

Height in miles
- 120

Ionosphere

50

Mesophere

30

Stratosphere

9

Troposphere

0

The weight of the atmosphere pushing down on the earth is called air pressure. Air pressure is greater nearer the surface of the earth because there is more air pushing down from above.

▲ The atmosphere is more than a hundred miles thick and is arranged in layers. The layer nearest the earth is about 9 miles deep and is called the troposphere. It contains nearly all the air and water vapor in the atmosphere. It is where changes in the atmosphere occur.

▲ Air pressure patterns in the atmosphere are changing all the time. With these changes come variations in the weather. A barometer shows changes in air pressure and what kind of weather to expect.

SUN RAYS

The sun's rays travel through the ▶ atmosphere. They warm the air and the surface of the land and sea. Heat from the land and sea then helps warm the air around us. Some heat escapes back into space, but a lot is trapped in the atmosphere and keeps the earth warm. This is known as the greenhouse effect.

Not all parts of the world receive the same amount of the sun's heat. Because the earth is round, the sun's rays come through the atmosphere and strike the curved surface at different angles. Areas near the equator get the sun's direct rays all year round, and so are very warm. Near the poles, though, the rays have to travel farther through the atmosphere before striking the earth's surface. Much of the heat is absorbed by the atmosphere, and when the rays do reach the earth, they are spread thin over a wide area. ▼

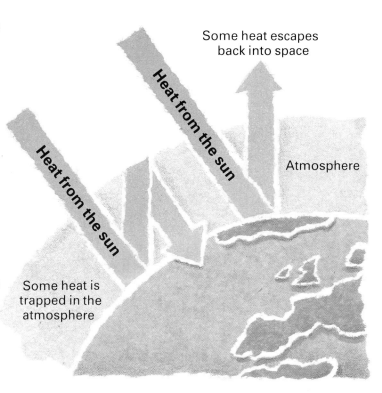

Position on the earth's surface is not the only factor that influences the temperature of a place. Winds and ocean currents may cool land down or bring in warm air. The higher the altitude of a place, the cooler it is likely to be. The amount of cloud cover will have an effect, too, and temperatures will usually be warmer in the day than at night. Weather fronts passing over can bring warm or cold air masses with them.

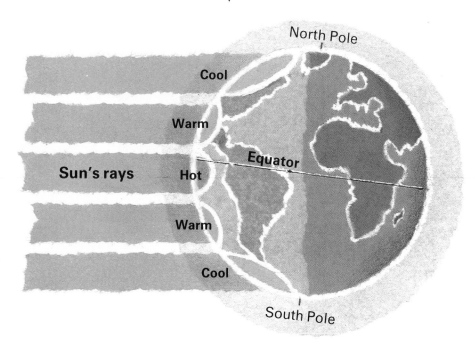

CLIMATE

Climate is defined by the regular weather patterns that an area has over a long period of time. The kind of climate a place has will be influenced by winds, ocean currents, height of the land, amount of sunlight reaching the place, and many other factors.

Regions of the world are often described according to the kind of climate they have. Usually they are described in terms of their temperature and rainfall patterns. There are many climates, but three main kinds will be discussed here. ▼

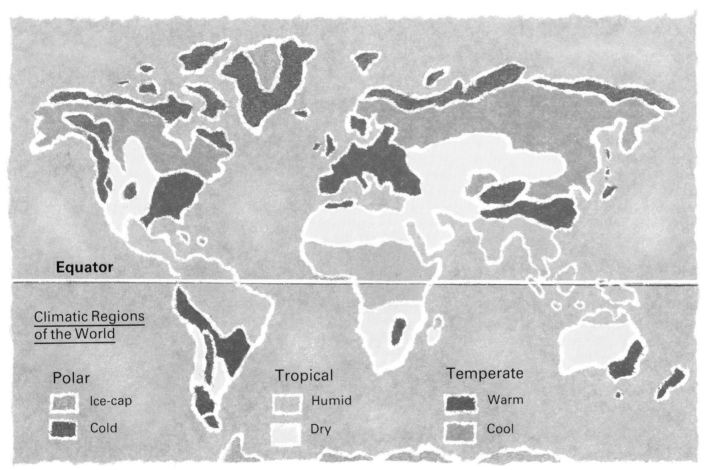

Equator

Climatic Regions of the World

Polar		Tropical		Temperate	
Ice-cap		Humid		Warm	
Cold		Dry		Cool	

Lands around the equator are usually hot all year round and have high rainfall. They are said to have a tropical climate.

The polar climate of the Arctic and Antarctic is much colder and often has snow all year round, even during the summer.

Between the equator and the poles there are many different types of climate. The regions that are said to have a temperate climate generally have summers that are warm and dry and winters that are cold and wet.

MOVING AIR

Warm air is lighter than cold air, ▶ so it rises. This is why hot air balloons float up into the sky. Air that has been warmed by the sun will also rise. Sometimes you can see birds spiraling upward on these moving air currents.

Warm air rising up into the atmosphere leaves behind an area of low pressure. Cooling as it rises, the air becomes heavy again and eventually sinks back downward, making an area of high pressure.

The sun heats the earth's surface unevenly. This creates recognizable zones of high and low pressure around the globe. ▶

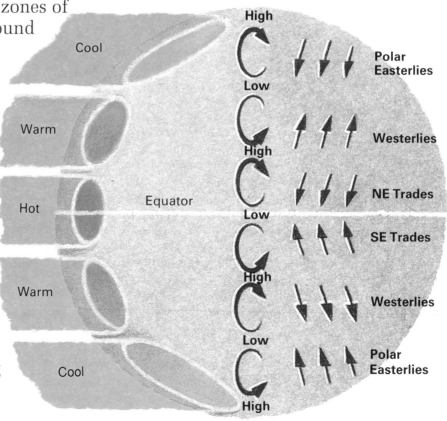

Wind is simply the ▶ movement of air over the surface of the earth. Air is always being pushed out of high pressure areas and sucked into low pressure areas.

As a result, the world ▶ has prevailing, or regular, winds that blow between the pressure zones. Instead of blowing directly north or south as you might expect, the moving air is thrown off course by the spin of the earth.

Cool
High
Low
Polar Easterlies

Warm
Low
High
Westerlies

Hot
Equator
High
Low
NE Trades

Warm
Low
SE Trades
High

Cool
Low
High
Westerlies

Polar Easterlies

1 The sun heats the earth unevenly.

2 Areas of high and low pressure are created.

3 Winds move from high to low pressure.

PRESSURE CHANGES

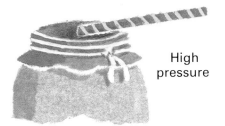

High pressure

Low pressure

There are two main types of barometer: mercury and aneroid. A mercury barometer measures air pressure by the height of the mercury in a long thin tube. An aneroid barometer works by the movement of a flexible skin over a sealed drum. High pressure causes the skin to flex inward and low pressure makes it bulge outward.

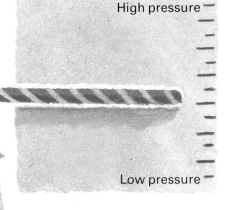

High pressure

Low pressure

Make a Simple Aneroid Barometer

1 Cut the neck off a balloon.
2 Stretch it tightly over a wide-necked jar and slip a rubber band or some thin string around it to hold the balloon tight.
3 Glue the end of a straw onto the center of the balloon.

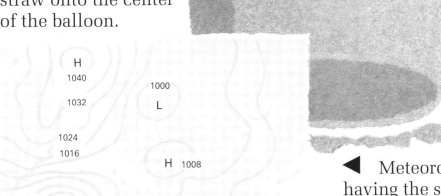

4 Draw a scale on a piece of paper marked from high to low and fix this behind the end of the straw.
5 Over a number of days, watch the straw move up and down as the air pressure changes.

◄ Meteorologists can link places having the same air pressure with lines called "isobars." Because the isobars are drawn in at regular millibar intervals, a weather map can quickly show us the changes in air pressure. Isobars that are close together mean air pressure is changing dramatically and with this comes strong winds, whereas an area with isobars far apart will be calm.

H
1040
1000
1032
L
1024
1016
H   1008
992
984   968
L
1000
1016   1008
1016

Isobar

9

WINDY WEATHER

The sun's heat creates patterns of air pressure and winds in a local area as well as on a global scale.

Land always heats up and cools down more quickly than water. Because of this, hot places near the sea often have winds that vary with night and day.

▲ As the land heats air above it during the day, the warm air rises and low pressure is created. Air is sucked in from over the sea and a cool sea breeze is felt.

▲ At night, the sea is still slowly releasing its heat and warming the air above it. A cool land breeze blows out to sea.

The Beaufort Scale

Force	Name of wind	Speed
0-1	Calm to light	0-3 mph
Description: Chimney smoke rises upward or drifts slightly.		
2-3	Gentle breeze	4-12 mph
Description: Soft wind on your face. Leaves and twigs sway gently on the trees.		
4-5	Fresh breeze	13-24 mph
Description: Dust and trash blow along the ground. Small trees bend.		
6-7	Strong breeze	25-31 mph
Description: Big trees sway and branches toss. Laundry on the line flaps.		
8-9	Gale	32-46 mph
Description: Branches snap on trees. Tiles fall from roofs. Wind is hard to walk into.		
10-11	Storm	47-75 mph
Description: People can be blown over and trees uprooted. Chimneys collapse and sheds blow over.		
12	Hurricane	Over 75 mph
Description: Houses blow down. Cars and trucks are tossed about.		

◄ At the beginning of the nineteenth century, Sir Francis Beaufort, a British admiral, worked out a scale to estimate wind speed. It is based on things that can be seen moving.

The Beaufort scale is still used today to describe wind speed. An anemometer can be used to measure the wind's speed more accurately.

Make a Weather Vane

1 Draw a large circle on cardboard. Mark the points of the compass on it.

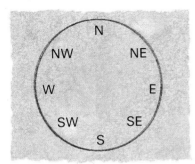

2 Use modeling clay to fix a plastic pot in the middle of the circle and glue a cork to the top of the pot.

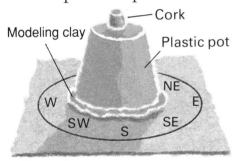

3 Cut two triangles of cardboard. Make one larger than the other.

4 Make slits in each end of a straw. Fit the triangles into the slits and glue them. Use the larger triangle for the tail and the smaller one for the pointer.

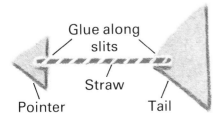

▲ A weather vane, like this one, is used to find out the direction of the wind.

5 Push a pin through the middle of the straw and then into the cork.

6 Place the weather vane outside. Use a compass or the sun to set it up in the right direction. (The sun rises in the east and sets in the west.) The wind vane will point in the direction the wind is coming from. A southerly wind will make the arrows point northward.

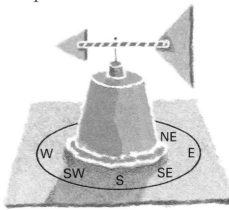

You can record your findings on a wind rose.

7 Mark the points of the compass around the edge of a piece of paper.

8 Draw a small circle in the middle.

9 Draw rows of squares from the edge of the circle to the compass points.

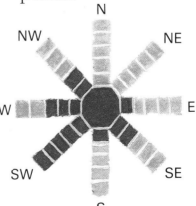

10 Each day, fill in a square on the wind rose to record the direction of the wind.

THE WATER CYCLE

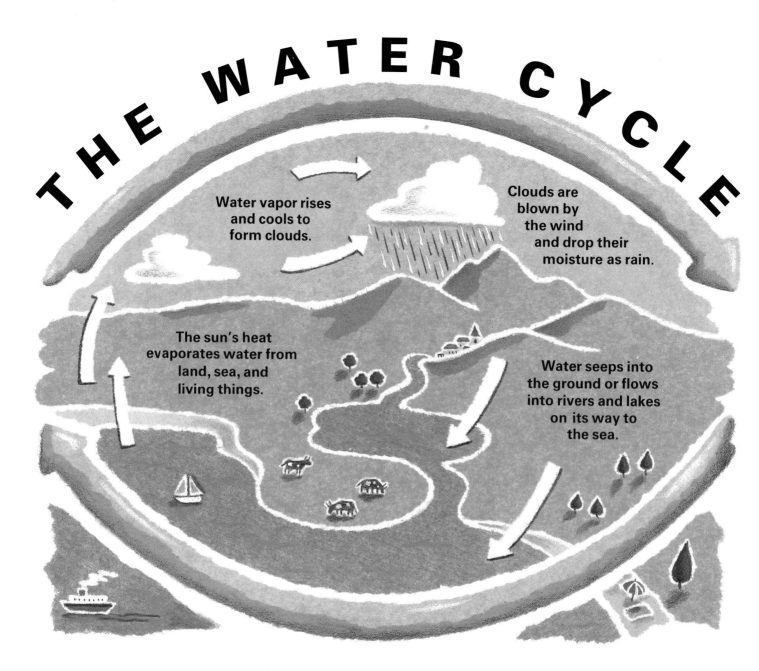

Water vapor rises and cools to form clouds.

Clouds are blown by the wind and drop their moisture as rain.

The sun's heat evaporates water from land, sea, and living things.

Water seeps into the ground or flows into rivers and lakes on its way to the sea.

There is a lot of water on earth. Most of it is salt water in the seas and oceans, and only a small amount is fresh water in lakes, rivers, and underground caverns. The water cycle keeps water changing between salt and fresh water. It keeps all living things supplied with the water they need.

Heat from the sun changes water from oceans and lakes into an invisible gas called water vapor. This process is called evaporation and it takes place all the time. The water vapor rises in the atmosphere, leaving any salt in the water behind. Watch the steam from a kettle to see how water vapor rises.

As air rises to higher altitudes, it expands and cools. This makes the water vapor condense into water droplets, which we see as clouds. Rain, snow, or hail may fall, bringing fresh water back to earth again. Most of the water that falls over the land runs back to the seas and the water cycle starts all over again.

DEW POINT

If you are out on a damp, misty morning, you might see dewdrops hanging from spiders' webs. During the night, moist air near the ground cools. Sometimes the air reaches a point when it can hold no more water vapor. This is known as dew point. The water vapor turns into tiny droplets of water. These settle on grass, twigs, and spiders' webs as dew.

On cold, clear nights dew point ▶ can be below freezing point, which is 32° Fahrenheit, (32°F). The air cools rapidly and the water vapor forms into tiny ice crystals. Everything is covered in sparkling frost.

▲ If the tiny water droplets are very fine, they may hang in the air as mist or fog. They can make it difficult to see into the distance.

DAMP AIR

There is always water in the air around us, even when we can't see it as mist or fog. The exact amount of water depends on the temperature of the air. Warm air holds more water vapor than cold. When we can feel the moisture in warm air, we say the weather is humid.

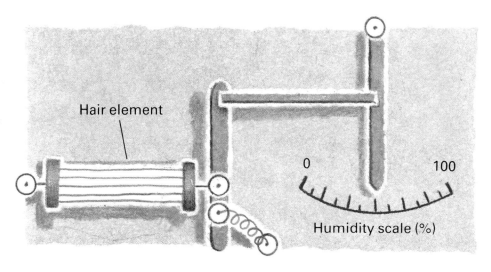

Hair element

0   100

Humidity scale (%)

Meteorologists can actually measure the humidity, or dampness, of the air by using instruments called hygrometers.

▲ Mechanical hygrometers use hair, which stretches when wet and shrinks when dry, to move a needle on a scale

Make a Coil Hygrometer

1 Cut a strip of cardboard about 1/2 in wide and 8 in long, with a flap at one end.
2 Roll the cardboard into a spiral.

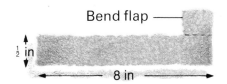

Bend flap

½ in

8 in

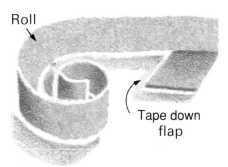

Roll

Tape down flap

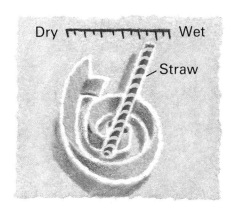

Dry ⊓⊓⊓⊓⊓⊓ Wet

Straw

3 Bend the flap and attach it to a large piece of cardboard. Don't let the spiral touch the cardboard.
4 Tape a straw to the end of the spiral.

5 Stand the hygrometer somewhere warm and dry, like over a radiator, for a few minutes. When the pointer begins to move, mark the direction with an arrow and label this "dry." Mark the opposite direction with an arrow and label this "wet."
6 Now leave your hygrometer in the place where you want to measure the humidity. The spiral will curl and uncurl slightly as the humidity changes.

CLOUD COVER

Clouds, like mist or fog, are actually millions of tiny water droplets, and sometimes ice crystals too. Clouds are formed when water vapor rises into the sky and then cools. The moisture may fall from the clouds as anything from a fine drizzle to a heavy downpour of rain.

If you watch the clouds, you will never see two quite the same; they are always changing their shape. Even so, there are ways of defining different types of clouds. In 1803, a meteorologist named Luke Howard was the first to classify clouds by the way they look. He separated them into cirrus (meaning a tuft of hair), cumulus (meaning a heap or pile), and stratus (meaning a flat layer). They are still described this way today, as well as by the altitude at which they are usually found. ▶

Clouds at all levels usually occur at weather fronts. Enormous patches of warm and cold air, called air masses, form over the earth's surface. Because of air pressure differences, warm and cold air masses don't mix when they meet. They form weather fronts instead. The warm air is pushed up into the sky and clouds appear as it rises and cools.

WOW!
The highest rainfall recorded for one day is 74.8 in on Reunion Island in the Indian Ocean on March 16, 1952.

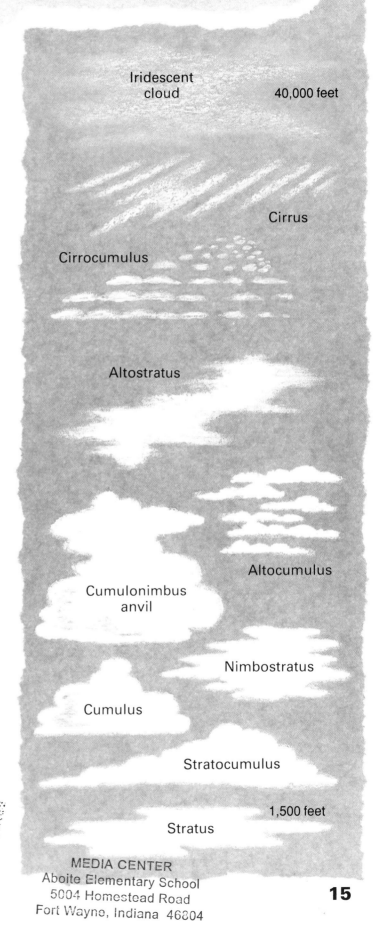

Iridescent cloud

40,000 feet

Cirrus

Cirrocumulus

Altostratus

Altocumulus

Cumulonimbus anvil

Nimbostratus

Cumulus

Stratocumulus

1,500 feet

Stratus

THUNDER AND LIGHTNING

In early times, people believed that the flash of lightning and rumble of thunder were signs of the gods' anger. Now we know that they are simply electrical storms.

There are about sixteen million thunderstorms a year around the world. Very often they come from dark cumulonimbus clouds that sit near the ground and stretch right up into the sky in the shape of a blacksmith's anvil.

Water droplets and ice crystals in a thunder cloud are tossed around by movements of air. One theory says these drops rub together and cause the cloud to become electrically charged. When the electrical charge is great enough, it streaks between clouds or to earth as a brilliant flash of lightning.

As the electricity travels, it makes the air around it expand very quickly. This violent movement of air creates the loud clap of thunder. When the storm is far away, the thunder rolls and rumbles as the sound is bounced between clouds. Although thunder and lightning occur at the same time, we see lightning before we hear the thunder because light travels faster than sound.

Sometimes objects on the ground may be struck by lightning and burn, but usually thunderstorms sound more dangerous than they really are.

VIOLENT STORMS

Hurricanes and tornadoes are storms that can leave behind paths of destruction and cause loss of life.

Hurricanes build up over the warm seas of the Caribbean and the southeastern coast of North America. The sun beats down on the sea and evaporates large quantities of water. Warm, moist air rises in the atmosphere creating a large depression, or area of very low air pressure. Air is sucked in quickly to replace the rising air. A whirlpool of hot, moist air spirals around the calm center.

▲ The hurricane grows bigger and stronger as it travels across the sea. It may measure 1,000 miles across and reach wind speeds of 180 mph.

◄ Tornadoes, like this one over Oklahoma, are smaller than hurricanes but their winds can reach 300 mph. They are also powered by rising humid air. The moisture condenses into water droplets so that the storm can be seen, usually as a twisting funnel shape. Tornadoes have the strength to lift heavy objects like cars and rooted trees.

WOW!
In Bedfordshire, England, in May 1950, a tornado is said to have plucked the feathers off several chickens. Surprisingly, they survived their ordeal.

ICE COLD

What would you pack in your suitcase for a vacation on a mountain top? Would you take a T-shirt and shorts, expecting it to be warm up nearer the sun? In fact, being nearer the sun means the weather is colder. The thin air cannot hold as much heat as air under greater pressure, so it cools as it rises up from lower areas.

Snow can fall at sea level, too, if the air is cold enough. If water in clouds is below 32° F, it turns into tiny ice crystals. Lots of ice crystals stick together to make snowflakes. When they fall through warm air, they usually turn to rain. But if they pass through cold air, fat flakes of snow will reach the ground.

▲ Some of the earth's highest mountain peaks in the Himalayas near the equator are covered in ice and snow all year round.

Ice crystals don't always fall as snowflakes. Sometimes, strong winds within cumulonimbus clouds may carry raindrops up to where the air is freezing. The raindrops freeze and fall where they pick up more water. They are then blown back up to where the water freezes. The cycle repeats and the frozen drops are like yo-yos. Each cycle, the ice ball becomes bigger. When the ice balls become too heavy for the wind to lift, they fall as hailstones.

▲ Hailstones can be as small as peas, but they may grow to be much larger. This photograph shows a thin section of a grapefruit-sized hailstone. It crashed to Earth in Kansas in 1970. Notice the layers that make up the hailstone. Hailstones can damage crops and buildings. The biggest stones are big enough to kill humans and other animals.

Have you ever made an ice slide on ▶ your playground? By rubbing and polishing the ice, you can make it very smooth and slippery. Smooth surfaces create less friction, or grip, so that when you step onto the ice, the bottom of your shoe will keep sliding along. In really cold weather, ponds sometimes freeze over. Ponds don't freeze evenly, and you can fall through weak spots. Always be sure that the ice is strong enough before you go onto it.

CHANGING SEASONS

In parts of the world that have a temperate climate, you could expect to be able to toboggan in the cold of winter and go picnicking on warm summer days.

The seasons of the ▶ world's temperate zones are caused by the tilting of the earth and the earth's orbiting around the sun and tilting at an angle to it. Seasons change as each half of the earth leans nearer to or farther from the sun. When it is summer in the Northern Hemisphere it is winter in the Southern Hemisphere. Spring and autumn mark the changes from winter to summer and back again.

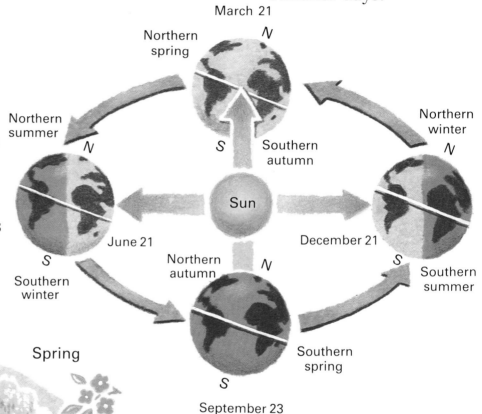

March 21
Northern spring
N
S
Southern autumn

Northern summer
N
S
Southern winter
June 21

Sun

Northern winter
N
S
Southern summer
December 21

Northern autumn
N
S
Southern spring
September 23

Winter

Spring

Autumn

Summer

◀ The changing of trees, shrubs, and small flowering plants often marks the changing seasons. New leaves and flowers appear as the air begins to warm in spring. Fruit grows, fattens, and ripens during the summer. In autumn, many soft-leaved plants die. Deciduous trees change color and lose their leaves before the cold of winter can harm them. The winter landscape can look bare and lifeless, but the plants are ready to spring to life when the weather warms again.

MIGRATION

Some species of birds and animals migrate with the seasons. They search out rich sources of food in new parts of the world.

Some insect-eating birds follow the sunshine. Wheatears breed in Greenland in the northern summer when insects are plentiful. As autumn arrives and daylight shortens, these tiny birds fly south to find food and avoid the long cold winter in the Arctic. They fly nearly 2,000 miles over the sea from Greenland to the northern coast of Spain without a rest. Many continue their journey southward to Africa. Others spend the winter in Britain or North America. ▼

▲ In the grassland area of the savannah in East Africa, seasonal changes are marked by dry and rainy periods. Vast herds of gazelle, zebra, and wildebeest move 125 miles between the Serengeti in the southeast and the Masai Mara in the northwest. They are in search of fresh green grass brought by the seasonal rains in each area.

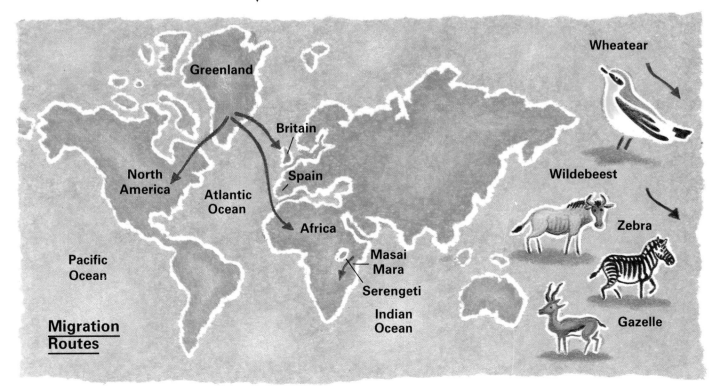

21

TIME AND CHANGE

Every plant and animal on earth has developed, or evolved, over millions of years to suit the climate in which they live. Their behavior, and even the way their bodies work, have adapted or are adapting to their surroundings.

Some animals simply hide themselves away in the cold winter months. They eat plenty of food during the summer in order to have large reserves of energy to live on. They find a snug hole or nest to fall asleep in until the weather warms up again.

◄ Sometimes animal behavior finds its way into weather lore. In the United States, February 2 is Groundhog Day . This is when the groundhog is said to come out of its long winter sleep. If the weather is cloudy and the groundhog doesn't see its shadow, it decides that spring is here and stays above ground. If it's sunny, it goes back into hibernation for another six weeks of winter.

Mammals living in temperate and polar areas grow thick coats to keep themselves warm in winter.

Weasels, like this one, ► snowshoe hares, and Arctic foxes grow white coats in winter to camouflage them against the snow. In spring they lose their thick hair and a brown coat grows to match the summer landscape. They can find just enough food to keep them going throughout the winter.

Plants have evolved to suit the climates in which they grow. In temperate regions their life cycles fit in with the seasons. They grow and reproduce during the warmer months and rest during the colder ones.

In the hot and humid climate of the equatorial rainforests, the weather is the same all year round. Plants can be found at any stage of their life cycles at any time.

Many plants growing in hot, dry deserts have incredibly long roots that can reach down to water deep beneath the surface. Often their leaves and skins are thick and waxy to stop precious water inside them from escaping.

▲ Some plants in deserts survive by fitting most of their life cycle into a short time after it has rained. The spring rains have brought brief color to this California desert.

PEOPLE AND WEATHER

People have to adapt to the weather too. Take a look at the traditional clothes of people from around the world. The Innuit of the Arctic wear warm furs, while the forest dwellers of the Amazon jungle need to wear very little. ▶

◀ People living in the mountains in Morocco in northern Africa keep themselves well-wrapped up. Their long, thick clothes keep out the scorching heat of day and the bitter cold of night. Their houses have thick mud walls and tiny windows for the same reasons.

Houses in warm, humid lands very often don't have solid walls and roofs. Air is allowed in to cool down the houses. In the hot, sticky climate of Pakistan, many homes are built with traps on the roof to catch wind and direct it down through the building.

Houses in cold climates need to be kept snug and warm. They are closed in with windows, doors, and solid walls. Very often their roofs are insulated with fluffy material to keep heat from being lost.

WOW!
In the cold Faeroes, north of Scotland, grass is grown on the roofs of the houses. This is a traditional way of insulating against heat loss.

WEATHERING

Rain, wind, frost, and ice are continually changing the surface of our earth. We call these changes to the land weathering. Weathering is a very slow process. From the moment a mountain is formed by the earth's movements it is attacked by the weather. Over millions of years, a jagged mountain peak will wear down.

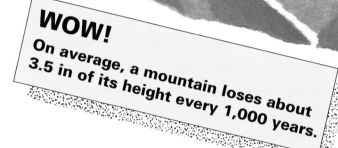

WOW!
On average, a mountain loses about 3.5 in of its height every 1,000 years.

Rain collects in cracks in rocks. If the weather freezes, the water expands. The ice can push apart the cracks in rocks like a wedge. Small pieces of rock, called scree, break off and often form a slope of loose material.

Wind can pick up tiny pieces of sand and throw it against rocks. It acts like a sandblaster: the rough edges of rocks are made smooth and round.

◀ In hot deserts there is no cloud cover to protect the land from changing temperatures. Rocks bake during the day and freeze at night. This makes them expand and shrink. The outer layers of rock flake off like an onion peel.

WOW!
Travelers in the desert say that cracking rocks make sounds like gun shots.

▲ The Devil's Marbles in Northern Territory, Australia, are a good example of "onion skin" weathering.

PREDICTING THE WEATHER

Some people look for signs around them and use old weather lore to predict the weather. Animal behavior is said to give clues about what the weather will do. Frogs are supposed to begin to croak and sheeps' wool is said to uncurl before rain. Some plants, like sunflowers, only open in fine weather and close up before a shower. Some people keep a piece of seaweed, which is hard and brittle in dry weather but becomes limp and floppy when rain is coming.

Modern weather forecasts are based on hundreds of measurements taken throughout the day. Weather stations, both on land and at sea, record temperature, rainfall, humidity, air pressure, and the speed and direction of the wind.

Weather balloons carry measuring instruments into the air to gather information about the atmosphere. The readings are sent back in the form of radio waves.

WOW!
In parts of Provence in France, farmers used to keep green tree frogs under glass bells. Their croaking warned the farmers of coming rain.

In many places you will see a white box, called a Stevenson's screen, that contains weather-recording instruments. Air humidity and temperature are being recorded from this one near Mombasa, Kenya. ▼

Weather	Instruments	Units	Weather	Instruments	Units
Atmospheric pressure	Aneroid barometer	millibars	Sunshine	Campbell Stokes recorder	hours
Temperature	Thermometer	°F	Wind speed	Anemometer	mph
Rainfall	Rain gauge	in	Humidity	Wet-bulb thermometer	°F

WEATHER
TECHNOLOGY

Detailed records from weather instruments have survived from as early as the seventeenth century. But it was not until 1850 that weather instruments became accurate enough to give information that could be used for forecasting. The electric telegraph, invented in 1844 by Samuel Morse, made it easy to collect readings quickly from long distances. This invention made the development of weather forecasting easier.

Meteorologists can now gather more information than ever by using modern technology. Satellites orbiting Earth collect weather information. They can show weather patterns that cannot be seen from Earth. Satellites can even measure wind speeds at sea level.

▲ All the information from weather stations, weather balloons, satellites, and radar is fed into computers to form a picture of how the weather is changing. But there are so many different things that influence the weather that forecasts can sometimes be inaccurate.

▲ The world's surface temperatures on a typical January day, put together from satellite data. Can you see the earth's main climatic zones (see page 7)?

CHANGING THE WEATHER

In 1946, scientists discovered that dropping tiny particles into some types of cloud could make them release rain. This became known as cloud seeding and has since been used in the United States, Russia, Australia, and France. Similar methods have been used to break up fog at busy airports. In the United States, cloud seeding has also been used to try and reduce lightning in storms, and in Russia it has been used to reduce the size of damaging hailstones.

Scientists would like to control the weather to help avoid natural disasters such as flooding or drought. But do they really know enough about the weather to be able to do this?

People have always wanted to be able to control the weather. Many peoples have special dances to encourage rain to fall in times of drought. Papuan mythology teaches that carrying grass during a rain dance pierces the eye of the sun, causing it to weep and be covered with clouds.

This dragon is a nineteenth-century Chinese symbol of life-bringing rain. The Dragon-Kings were called upon in times of drought or to stop flooding.

The earth's climate has changed and shifted many times during its history. As little as 10,000 years ago, a permanent layer of ice was only just disappearing from northern Europe and North America as the Ice Age ended. Scientists have discovered that today's temperatures are still colder than those of millions of years ago.

People are worried that modern lifestyles are changing the world's weather. The earth is surrounded by gases in the atmosphere that act like a blanket, stopping the sun's warmth traveling back out into space (see page 6 - the greenhouse effect).

The burning of fossil fuels for energy to heat homes, run cars, and keep factories working releases the gas carbon dioxide into the atmosphere. The amount of carbon dioxide in the atmosphere is increasing, so more heat is being trapped.

Scientists are unsure what effects this global warming will have on the world's weather. There may be more extremes of weather, such as drought, flooding, and hurricanes. The world's major climatic zones may even move slightly.

▲ Weather disasters, like this flood in Mauras, India, and changes in the earth's climate are more likely to affect the poorer countries of the world. They cannot afford to take measures against the weather.

GLOSSARY

Air mass A large body of warm or cold air.

Air pressure The weight of the atmosphere pressing down on the earth's surface.

Altitude Height above sea level.

Anemometer An instrument that measures wind speed.

Aneroid Containing or using no liquid.

Atmosphere The layers of air around the earth.

Barometer An instrument that measures air pressure.

Beaufort scale A scale used to measure the force of the wind. It is based on observation of the effects of the wind on everyday objects.

Climate General weather patterns experienced in a place over a long period of time.

Condense To change from a gas into a liquid. The opposite process of evaporation.

Depression An area of low air pressure.

Dew point The temperature at which dew forms when water condenses out of air.

Electrical charge A buildup of positive or negative electrical particles.

Evaporate To change from a liquid into a gas. Water changes to water vapor.

Expand To grow larger.

Freezing point The temperature at which liquid turns solid. Water turns into a solid–ice–at 32° on the Fahrenheit scale.

Humidity The amount of water vapor in the air.

Hygrometer An instrument that measures humidity.

Ice crystals Tiny regularly shaped ice.

Insulation A material that slows the passage of heat. Insulation can be used to keep things warm or cold.

Isobar A line, drawn on a weather chart, that joins points of the same air pressure.

Mercury A silver-white poisonous metallic liquid used in barometers and thermometers.

Meteorologist A scientist who studies the atmosphere and weather.

Millibar A unit of atmospheric pressure.

Radar A piece of equipment that uses radio waves to transmit pictures or sounds.

Water Vapor Water that is held in the air in the form of a gas.

Weather front Where different air masses meet, usually bringing unsettled weather.

Weathering The effect of the weather in breaking down rocks.

Weather lore Weather sayings, myths and legends.

BOOKS TO READ

You can explore lots of topics from this book, but here is a list of other books about weather to get you started.

Adler, David. *World of Weather*. Mahwah, NJ: Troll, 1983.
Armbruster, Ann and Elizabeth A. Taylor. *Tornadoes*. New York: Franklin Watts, 1989
Barrett, Norman. *Hurricanes and Tornadoes*. New York: Franklin Watts, 1990
Bramwell, Martyn. *Weather*. New York: Bookwright Press, 1987
Cosner, Shaaron. *Be Your Own Weather Forecaster*. New York: Julian Messner, 1981
Dineen, Jacqueline. *Hurricanes and Typhoons*. New York: Gloucester Press, 1991
Flint, David. *Weather and Climate*. New York: Gloucester Press, 1991
Ford, Adam. *Weather Watch*. New York: Lothrop, Lee & Shepard, 1982
Gibbons, Gail. *Weather Forecasting*. New York: Four Winds, 1987
Kelly, Janet. *Be Your Own Weather Expert*. New York: Simon & Schuster, 1991
Mason, John. *Autumn Weather*. New York: Bookwright Press, 1991
             Spring Weather. New York: Bookwright Press, 1991
             Summer Weather. New York: Bookwright Press, 1991
             Winter Weather. New York: Bookwright Press, 1991
Nattan, Louis J. *Weather*. Englewood Cliffs, NJ: Prentice Hall, 1985
Pettigrew, Mark. *Weather*. New York: Gloucester Press, 1987
Sabin, Louis. *Weather*. Mahwah, NJ: Troll, 1985
Steel, Phillip. *Storms: Causes and Effects*. New York: Franklin Watts 1991
             Wind: Causes and Effects. New York: Franklin Watts 1991
Taylor, Barbara. *Wind and Weather*. New York: Franklin Watts, 1991
Taylor-Cork, Barbara. *Be an Expert Weather Forecaster*. New York: Gloucester Press, 1992

INDEX

Air 5, 6, 8, 10, 13, 14, 15, 16, 17, 18, 20, 24, 26
  currents 8
  masses 6, 15,
  pressure 5, 8, 9, 10, 12, 17, 18, 26
Altitude 6, 15
Anemometers 10
Antarctic 7
Arctic 7, 21, 22, 24
Atmosphere 4, 5, 6, 8, 12, 17, 26, 29
Australia 25, 28

Barometers 5, 9
Beaufort scale 10

Carbon dioxide 5, 29
Climates 7, 22, 23, 24, 27, 29
  polar 7, 22
  temperate 7, 20, 22, 23
  tropical 7, 23
Clothes 24
Clouds 4, 6, 12, 15, 16, 18, 19, 22, 25, 28
Cloud seeding 28

Depression 17
Deserts 23, 25
Dew point 13
Drought 28, 29

Equator, the 6, 7, 18, 23
Europe 29
Evaporation 12
Evolution 22, 23

Flooding 28, 29
Fog 4, 13, 14, 15, 28
France 28

Freezing point (32° F) 13, 18
Frost 4, 13, 25

Global warming 29
Greenhouse effect 6, 29
Groundhog Day 22

Hail 12, 19, 28
Hibernation 22
Houses 24
Humidity 14, 17, 23, 24, 26
Hurricanes 10, 17, 29
Hygrometers 14

Ice 18, 19, 25, 29
  crystals 13, 15, 16, 18, 19, 25, 29
Ice Age, the 29
India 29
Insulation 24
Isobars 9

Kenya 26

Meteorologists 9 14, 15, 27
Migration 21
Mist 13, 14, 15

Ocean currents 6, 7

Plants 20, 22, 23, 26
Poles, the 6, 7
Pressure (see air pressure)
Rain 4, 7, 12, 15, 18, 19, 21, 23, 25, 26, 28
Rainforests 23, 24
Russia 28

Satellites 27
Seasons 7, 20, 21, 23
  autumn 20, 21
  rainy 21
  spring 20, 22
  summer 7, 20, 21, 22
  winter 7, 20, 21, 22
Snow 7, 12, 18, 19, 22
Stevenson's screen 26
Sun 4, 6, 7, 8, 10, 11, 12, 17, 18, 20, 28, 29

Temperature 6, 7, 12, 14, 26, 27, 29
Thunderstorms 4, 16, 28
Tornadoes 17
Troposphere 5

United States 17, 21, 22, 23, 26, 28, 29

Water 10, 12, 14
  cycle 12
  droplets 13, 15, 16
  vapor 5, 12, 13, 14, 15
Weather
  balloons 26
  forecasting 4, 26, 27
  fronts 6, 15
  lore 22, 26
  maps 4, 9
  mythology 28
  symbols 4
  vane 11
Weathering 25
Wind 4, 6, 7, 8, 9, 10, 11, 17, 19, 24, 25, 26
  rose 11
  speed 10, 17, 26